Experience God's Law of Attraction Through Bible Verses and Spiritual Affirmations

SUSAN LEE

The Produce My Book Promise:

Our goal at ProduceMyBook.com is to provide you with a proven sequence of steps and sub-steps to learn and apply new skills...faster.

Authors benefit from our process by having a completed book to call their own, in as little as 8 weeks, without ever typing a word of the manuscript.

c/o Produce My Book
PO Box 441024
Aurora, CO 80044
ProduceMyBook.com
crew@ProduceMyBook.com

CONTENTS

FREE BONUS

SUSAN LEE

FREE BONUS!

Thanks for downloading *Experiencing God's Law of Attraction Through Bible Verses and Spiritual Affirmations*!

As a special gift for taking the time, I would like to provide you with access to **God's Law of Attraction Worksheets** which will help you determine your goals, create positive affirmations, and combat negative beliefs.

Also, you will receive two special collections, formatted for printing as reminder cards to be carried with you throughout the day:

Treasury of God's Promises is a collection of Bible verses that will help you focus on God's positive message.

Quotable Quotes is a selection of affirming quotes that will help you to keep God's powerful word in your heart.

To get all three gifts, just visit **ProduceMyBook.com/gloabonusreg**.

Now, on with *Experiencing God's Law of Attraction Through Bible Verses and Spiritual Affirmation*

1
INTRODUCTION

What, is the law of attraction? Some think it is little more than warm and fuzzy self-help jargon - and about as helpful as a pat on the back and a positive "you can do it!" But what if there is something more to it than positive cheerleading?

Others call it witchcraft, a "secret" ritual or spell you can learn that will magically bring you everything you ever wanted in life. But what if the law of attraction is much more natural and wholesome than witchcraft?

What if the law of attraction is really "God's law of attraction?"

The principles of "thought begets thought" and "for every action, there is a reaction" have been present throughout both ancient and modern history, which suggests that something happens when you apply the law. Common beliefs such as these become common because they work.

In the same way chemistry, logic, physics, weather patterns, and planetary motion exist, so too, does the law of attraction. It works in our lives, positively or negatively, regardless of our conscious awareness of its presence. As Christians, we shouldn't fear the law of attraction any more than we fear chemistry. It is a gift from God.

Simply, God's law of attraction can be described as "You attract into your life more of whatever you are giving your focus, attention, and energy to."

It can be bad things (normally attracted without your awareness) or good things (which can be deliberate or non-deliberate).

Our goal in practicing the law of attraction is to minimize the non-deliberate negative focus, attention, and energy (often described as "vibration") and replace it with positive. This positive focus, attention, and energy will most likely begin as deliberate, and as you can successfully practice the law of attraction, will evolve into a combination of deliberate and non-deliberate.

There are five basic steps for deliberately attracting more of the positive into your life and less of the negative: ASK, BELIEVE, ACT, ALLOW, AND RECEIVE. To learn more about each of these principles and how they fit into God's law of attraction, please read God's Law of Attraction: The Believer's Guide to Success and Fulfillment (learn more at ProduceMyBook.com).

One proven way to combat negative thoughts and vibrations is through the use of positive desire statements, which are often called affirmations. If you can build an arsenal of affirmations, the instant you feel resistance to a negative thought or situation you can dig for that positive statement and repeat it to yourself until positive vibrations overpower the negative ones.

God provides many of these positive statements in His Word. Using God's Word to create your affirmations only strengthens the positive vibrations in your life and increases the opportunities for you to fulfill God's purpose.

This guide is intended to point you toward many of the powerful verses in God's Word and provide sample affirmations that you can use to combat negative thinking. This guide is merely a starting point as the Bible is full of promises and positive messages that will speak directly to you. Always make it a part of your life to explore God's Word and claim it as your own.

I have broken this guide into six parts, one for each step of God's laws of attraction (ASK, BELIEVE, ACT, ALLOW AND RECEIVE), as well as one final section regarding positive mental attitude, the attitude that is so critical to successfully achieving God's plans for your life. My hope is that the Bible verses and affirmations found in this guide will bless you throughout your life.

To learn more about God's law of attraction and how it can help you to identify and achieve God's plan for your life, please read God's Law of Attraction: The Believer's Guide to Success and Fulfillment (Learn more at ProduceMyBook.com).

2
PART 1: ASK

Throughout the Bible, God encourages us to ask Him for what we want. But despite this, many of us have deep-rooted beliefs that wanting more is "bad," which results in apathetic acceptance of the status quo and hidden fear of changing. In other words, a silent acceptance of the negative vibes in our lives as normal and the belief that it is all we can or should expect.

The Asking step is critical in the law of attraction whether we are asking for something physical, or material (such as a new house) or something less tangible (such as being able to start a charity for a worthy cause).

Keep in mind that you are already asking for things all day long according to the principles of the law of attraction. Remember, whatever you put your focus, attention and energy into, is what you will attract into your life. It only makes sense to banish negative, self-deprecating "asks" and replace them with positive affirming ones.

We, as God's people have the distinct privilege to be able to ask God directly in prayer. Prayer is our way of establishing a real relationship with our heavenly Father. And, because we know that God wants every good thing that He has in store for us, we can pray confidently, knowing that whether the answer is "yes," "no" or "not yet," our prayers have been answered!

BIBLE VERSES AND AFFIRMATIONS - ASK

Job 11:18 Having hope will give you courage. You will be protected and will rest in safety.
Affirmation: I dream big dreams because I know God resides in my hope.

Leviticus 26:12 I will walk among you; I will be your God, and you will be my people.
Affirmation: I have a close relationship with God - I can come to Him with anything.

Mark 11:24 I tell you, you can pray for anything, and if you believe that you've received it, it will be yours.
Affirmation: I believe that with God, all things, including my dreams and goals, are possible.

1 Thessalonians 5:16-17 Always be joyful. Never stop praying.
Affirmation: I am so happy and thankful to be able to come to God with all my needs and wants.

Matthew 7:7 Keep on asking, and you will receive what you ask for. Keep on seeking, and you will find. Keep on knocking, and the door will be opened to you.
Affirmation: I am persistent in my prayers to achieve God's will. Satan's influence doesn't sway me, and I am not frustrated by the world's delays.

Psalm 107:28-30 "Lord, help!" they cried in their trouble, and he saved them from their distress. He calmed the storm to a whisper and stilled the waves. What a blessing was that stillness as he brought them safely into harbor!
Affirmation: I always go to God first, even in my troubles. When I lean on Him, he brings me peace and gives me hope again.

John 14:13-14 You can ask for anything in my name, and I will do it so that the Son can bring glory to the Father. Yes, ask me for anything in my name, and I will do it!
Affirmation: I gladly commit to and wait on the Lord, knowing that by asking earnestly in His name I will achieve His plans for me.

Ephesians 6:18 Pray in the Spirit at all times and on every occasion. Stay alert and be persistent in your prayers for all believers everywhere.
Affirmation: I am still and listen for the Spirit's guidance, and in following the Spirit's lead my prayers are pleasing to God.

James 5:16 Confess your sins to each other and pray for each other so that you may be healed. The earnest prayer of a righteous person has great power and produces wonderful results.
Affirmation: I confess my mistakes to the people I have hurt, and ask God to forgive me. When I come clean of my sins, God can work through me to achieve His plans.

Matthew 7:8 For everyone who asks, receives. Everyone who seeks finds. And to everyone who knocks, the door will be opened.
Affirmation: I am bold in asking God for what I need and want. I am ready to walk through the door when He opens

it.

Ephesians 3:12 Because of Christ and our faith in him, we can now come boldly and confidently into God's presence.
Affirmation: I pray to God with confidence! His grace has set me free!

1 John 5:14-15 And we are confident that he hears us whenever we ask for anything that pleases him. And since we know he hears us when we make our requests, we also know that he will give us what we ask for.
Affirmation: I pray boldly to God for what I want and need. Then I give it up to Him, knowing that if it is His will, I will receive it.

Psalm 4:1 Answer me when I call to you, O God, who declares me innocent. Free me from my troubles. Have mercy on me and hear my prayer.
Affirmation: I speak freely to God about my troubles as well as my victories, and he listens!

Matthew 6:6 But when you pray, go away by yourself, shut the door behind you, and pray to your Father in private. Then your Father, who sees everything, will reward you.
Affirmation: I spend private time with God praying and listening for His answers. My time with God isn't about impressing others but about building my relationship with Him.

Isaiah 55:6 Seek the Lord while you can find Him. Call on Him now while He is near.
Affirmation: I take every opportunity I can to draw closer to God. I pray to Him during my good times as well as my bad.

Matthew 21:22 You can pray for anything, and if you have faith, you will receive it.

Affirmation: While the world creates doubt, God is sure. With God, all is possible. God, I pray for the faith I need to believe in you!

3
PART 2: BELIEVE

Belief is tough. We may know that we want that new house, and even ask for it, but when we look at our bank account and the way our current house has depreciated, it's hard to believe it could ever happen.

We've been so conditioned to think that "seeing is believing." With God's law of attraction, the real secret is "believing is seeing."

Psalm 37: 5 reads: "Commit your way to the Lord; trust also in Him and He will bring it to pass." It doesn't say that you have to figure out "how" it will come to pass, only that you trust that, through God, it will. Remember, God created everything there is. Nothing exists that He didn't make (John 1: 3). If that is true, and we believe it, it should be easy to believe that nothing is impossible, even if we can't see how it could happen in the natural.

Developing a toolkit of positive affirmations related to

belief is an all important strategy for us to help strengthen our belief in all God can achieve through us. Here are some to get you started.

BIBLE VERSES AND AFFIRMATIONS - BELIEVE

2 Corinthians 9:8 God can pour on the blessings in astonishing ways so that you're ready for anything & everything, more than just ready to do what needs to be done.
Affirmation: Through God, I can be and do more than I ever could alone.

Deuteronomy 28:8 The Lord will bless everything you do and fill your storehouses with grain. The Lord, your God, will bless you in the land He is giving you.
Affirmation: God will provide all I need to fulfill His plan.

Hebrews 3:14 For if we are faithful to the end, trusting God as firmly as when we first believed, we will share in all that belongs to Christ.
Affirmation: I persevere to the end, I trust God for the strength to complete it, I never lose faith.

Matthew 9:29 Because of your faith, it will happen.
Affirmation: I have big prayers and dream big dreams because I have big faith that God will help me to achieve my goals.

Philippians 4:6 Don't worry about anything; instead pray about everything. Tell God what you need, and thank Him for all He has done.
Affirmation: I gladly trust God with everything.

Proverbs 3:5-6 Trust in the Lord with all your heart; do not depend on your own understanding. Seek His will in all you do, and He will direct your path.

Affirmation: I honor God's will in all I do, and He gives me all I need to succeed.

Revelation 21:7 All who are victorious will inherit all these blessings, and I will be their God, and they will be my children.

Affirmation: God's blessings are mine, and I am victorious in the Lord!

Hebrews 11:1 Faith is the confidence that what we hope for will actually happen; it gives us assurance about things we cannot see.

Affirmation: I don't have to see it to believe it because I know God works in the unseen.

Ephesians 2:8 God saved you by His grace when you believed. And you can't take credit for this; it is a gift from God.

Affirmation: It's not my job to figure out HOW. My only job is to believe.

1 Corinthians 16:3 Be on guard. Stand firm in the faith. Be courageous. Be strong.

Affirmation: I have the strength of God on my side! I am strong and courageous against the enemies of this world.

Matthew 17:20 "I tell you the truth, if you had faith even as small as a mustard seed, you could say to this mountain, 'Move from here to there,' and it would move. Nothing would be impossible.

Affirmation: Lord: Help me find the faith to move mountains. I know with You, nothing is impossible. Please help take me out of the picture, so I focus on you alone.

Romans 1:17 This Good News tells us how God makes us

right in His sight. This is accomplished from start to finish by faith. As the Scriptures say, "It is through faith that a righteous person has life."
Affirmation: I believe in God's power, not my power. I don't need to do anything but believe.

2 Corinthians 5:7 For we live by believing and not by seeing.
Affirmation: I believe God has big plans for my life, and I am ready!

John 20:29 Then Jesus told him, "You believe because you have seen me. Blessed are those who believe without seeing me."
Affirmation: I see all the wonderful things God has planned for my future and believe they will happen at just the right time.

Deuteronomy 7:9 Understand, therefore, that the Lord your God is indeed God. He is the faithful God who keeps His covenant for a thousand generations and lavishes His unfailing love on those who love Him and obey His commands.
Affirmation: I know that God loves me, and will take care of me always. Knowing this, I can be my best for God and work to achieve His plans for me.

Philippians 4:13 For I can do all things through Christ who give me strength!
Affirmation: I can do everything I need and want to do, through Christ, who gives me the strength I need.

Proverbs 16:3 Put God in charge of your work, then what you've planned will take place.
Affirmation: I commit my work to God. I don't need to know how it will happen, just work to His glory and He will

answer my prayers.

Ephesians 6:16 In addition to all of these, hold up the shield of faith to stop the fiery arrows of the devil.
Affirmation: I don't listen to the world that says "you can't." I hold up God's shield against those negative influences and declare out loud "I CAN!"

Matthew 9:22 Jesus turned around, and when he saw her He said, "Daughter, be encouraged! Your faith has made you well." And the woman was healed at that moment.
Affirmation: I am strong and healthy. I am well able to achieve God's plan!

4
PART 3: ACT

Just as the master in the story of the three servants (Matthew 25: 14-30) expected his servants to take action and invest his assets while he was gone; so too does God expects us to prepare ourselves for the good things to come into our lives.

If you have a goal that you truly feel God is calling you to achieve, you should commit to doing at least one thing each day toward achieving it. The one thing doesn't have to be big at all. Maybe it is just a matter of reading a bit in a trade journal for your ideal career field or fine-tuning your resume or calling an associate you haven't talked to in a while.

Provided that you aren't trying to control the situation over God, a little action is always better than no action. First, it helps remove doubt and resistance to your goal. Second, it is a way to respond to God's call with belief. You may have no idea how your little action will help you to achieve a seemingly impossible goal, but God can do the impossible.

Sometimes, our only action in a situation is to be able to discern what God is asking us to do. Once we know His will for our lives and just go with the flow, rather than worrying it to death or trying to manipulate the situation, He can achieve all the great things he has in store for us.

In God's law of attraction, it isn't enough to just "ask," "believe," and "receive." Action on our part is an important ingredient in attracting the good things God has in store for us. In addition to actively working to discern God's will in our lives, we also need to take the actions needed to set the wheels of our desire into process.

BIBLE VERSES AND AFFIRMATIONS - ACT

Colossians 3: 23 Whatever you do, work at it with all your heart, as working for the Lord, not for men.
Affirmation: I put my heart and soul into my work so that I may honor God in all I do.

Galatians 6:9 Don't get tired of doing what is good. Don't get discouraged and give up, for we will reap a harvest of blessing at the appropriate time.
Affirmation: I am responsible and get the jobs done I need to be done for the glory of God.

Isaiah 30:21 Your own ears will hear him. Right behind you a voice will say "This is the way you should go," whether to the right or to the left.
Affirmation: I consistently listen for God's direction in my life and take action in response to His guidance.

Luke 6: 38 Give, and you will receive. Your gift will return to you in full—pressed down, shaken together to make room for more, running over, and poured into your lap. The amount you give will determine the amount you get back.

Affirmation: I commit my whole self and all my resources to achieving God's best.

1 John 1:9 If we confess our sins, He is faithful and just and will forgive us our sins and purify us from all unrighteousness.

Affirmation: I will confess my sins to God - big and small, and accept His forgiveness; so that I can do His will and be ready for His blessings.

Joshua 1:9 This is my command—be strong and courageous. Do not be afraid or discouraged. For the Lord your God is with you wherever you go.

Affirmation: I am bold in my actions knowing that God is with me all the time.

Deuteronomy 31:6 So be strong and courageous! Do not be afraid and do not panic before them. For the Lord your God will personally go ahead of you. He will neither fail you nor abandon you.

Affirmation: I boldly take action toward God's plans for me even when I am afraid or uncertain because I know Jesus is with me every step of the way.

James 5: 7-8 Dear brothers and sisters, be patient as you wait for the Lord's return. Consider the farmers who patiently wait for the rains in the fall and in the spring. They eagerly look for the valuable harvest to ripen. You, too, must be patient. Take courage, for the coming of the Lord is near.

Affirmation: Sometimes, patience is all the action I need to achieve God's plans for me!

Romans 8:28 And we know that God causes everything to work together for the good of those who love God and are called according to His purpose for them.
Affirmation: When I am following God's call, I am happy knowing my actions will work together to help achieve His plan.

James 2: 14 What good is it, dear brothers and sisters, if you say you have faith but don't show it by your actions? Can that kind of faith save anyone?
Affirmation: I believe in God's plans for me, and take action every day toward achieving those goals.

Isaiah 32:17 The fruit of that righteousness will be peace; its effect will be quietness and confidence forever.
Affirmation: I feel peace and confidence when I listen to the Holy Spirit's guidance.

James 1:5 If any of you lacks wisdom, you should ask God, who gives generously to all without finding fault, and it will be given to you.
Affirmation: I study God's Word and find all the answers to my challenges.

Psalm 119:105 Your word is a lamp for my feet, and a light on my path.
Affirmation: I take time every day to hear God through His Word.

James 1: 25 If you look carefully into the perfect law that sets you free, and if you do what it says and don't forget what you heard, then God will bless you for doing it.
Affirmation: I listen carefully for God's direction and act on it every day.

James 2: 15-17 Suppose a brother or a sister is without

clothes and daily food. If one of you says to them, "Go in peace; keep warm and well fed," but does nothing about their physical needs, what good is it? In the same way, faith by itself, if it is not accompanied by action, is dead.

Affirmation: I never ignore God's call. I see what goes on around me, and take action to help those people that God has placed in my heart to help.

2 Peter 1: 5-8 In view of all this, make every effort to respond to God's promises. Supplement your faith with a generous provision of moral excellence, and moral excellence with knowledge, and knowledge with self-control, and self-control with patient endurance, and patient endurance with godliness, and godliness with brotherly affection, and brotherly affection with love for everyone. The more you grow like this, the more productive and useful you will be in your knowledge of our Lord Jesus Christ.

Affirmation: I excitedly wait for God's promises in my life. I persistently act toward achieving the goals he has placed in my heart.

5
PART 4: ALLOW

Regardless of how much you ask, believe, or act, the law of attraction can still go "wrong" if you fail to achieve Step 4 of the process and allow what you are attracting into your life. Most of the time we aren't consciously rejecting the attraction of these things, but we aren't allowing them to happen in our life, either.

The first thing that will prevent you from allowing your desires into your life is the presence of doubt and worry. The doubt, worry and fear we carry with us result in our resistance to believing good things will happen. And, the presence of that doubt, fear and worry cause negative vibrations.

The second thing that can keep you from allowing attraction into your life of your wants is, as Tony Robbins says, "your story as to why you can't get them." Others call this story your limiting beliefs.

There are a lot of definitions for limiting beliefs, but in a nutshell, a limiting belief is something that you believe to be true about yourself that is not true; and it prevents you from moving forward as you'd like. Remembering God's promises can help dispel these limiting beliefs.

BIBLE VERSES AND AFFIRMATIONS - ALLOW

1 Corinthians 10: 13 All you need to remember is that God will never let you down; he'll never let you be pushed past your limit; he'll always be there to help you come through it.
Affirmation: I thank you God for standing by me through it all. Please prepare me for your blessings.

Isaiah 40: 29-31 He gives power to those who are tired and worn out, He offers strength to the weak. Even youths will become exhausted & young men will give up. But those who wait on the Lord will find new strength. They will fly high on wings like eagles. They will run and not grow weary. They will walk and not faint.
Affirmation: I am strong and well able! I will fulfill God's plan for me! God gives me the strength I need every day, every hour, every minute to persevere to the end.

John 15:4 Remain in me, and I will remain in you. For a branch cannot produce fruit if it is severed from the vine, and you cannot be fruitful unless you remain in me.
Affirmation: I can do so much if I remain in God's strength. My failures come from trying to do it all myself.

Matthew 6: 31-33 Do not be anxious, saying "what shall we eat?" or "what shall we drink?" or "what shall we wear?" For the Gentiles seek after all these things, and your heavenly Father knows you need them all. But seek first the Kingdom of God and His righteousness, and all these things will be added to you.

Affirmation: I gladly put God first in everything I do, including overcoming my strongholds.

Isaiah 43:2 When you go through deep waters, I will be with you. When you go through rivers of difficulty, you will not drown. When you walk through the fire of oppression, you will not be burned up; the flames will not consume you.
Affirmation: I love knowing God has my back. I can risk anything He calls me to without worry or fear!

1 Peter 5:7 Give all your worries and cares to God, for He cares about you.
Affirmation: I don't worry about anything. God is in control and loves me.

Matthew 11:28 Then Jesus said, "Come to me, all of you who are weary and carry heavy burdens, and I will give you rest.
Affirmation: I am at peace, knowing that no matter how stressful or overwhelming a situation can be, God is with me and supporting me.

Isaiah 59:1 Listen! The Lord's arm is not too weak to save you, nor is His ear too deaf to hear your call.
Affirmation: No sin is too great for God to forgive - I will not hold onto my sins but will confess and give them all to God.

Psalm 55:22 Give your burdens to the Lord, and he will take care of you. He will not permit the godly to slip and fall.
Affirmation: God has my back. He's there through thick and thin. He'll catch me when I fall.

Philippians 1: 6 God never stops working in our lives.
Affirmation: I'm redeemed and forgiven! My best days are

ahead of me.

Proverbs 4: 20-21 Pay attention to what I say; listen closely to my words. Do not let them out of your sight, keep them within your heart.
Affirmation: I always stay focused on my goals. Because I know they are from God and for His glory, I am pursuing them until I succeed.

Psalm 60:12 With God's help we will do mighty things, for he will trample down our foes.
Affirmation: I don't fear anything or anybody because God is with me. With Him, I can achieve more than I could ever imagine.

Matthew 8:26 Jesus responded, "Why are you afraid? You have so little faith!" Then he got up and rebuked the wind and waves, and suddenly there was a great calm.
Affirmation: God calms all the storms in my life. There is nothing to be worried about because He is all powerful!

Luke 12:27-28 "Look at the lilies and how they grow. They don't work or make their clothing, yet Solomon in all his glory was not dressed as beautifully as they are. And if God cares so wonderfully for flowers that are here today and thrown into the fire tomorrow, he will certainly care for you. Why do you have so little faith?
Affirmation: God will take care of me and provide for my needs. I don't have to worry anymore!

Acts 17:28 For in Him we live and move and exist.
Affirmation: I live every day as a treasured child of God. In Him, I can do anything!

6
PART 5: RECEIVE

The final step in God's law of attraction process is to receive His blessings into your life.

Remember that regardless of whether good things or bad are happening in your life the law of attraction is at work. The purpose of learning to use the law of attraction is to work Steps 1-4 intentionally to allow more blessings into your life and less bad things.

It may seem like the final step, to "Receive," is a bit anti-climactic because usually you receive what you have attracted without band music, confetti and parades. It just happens. If you aren't aware of God and His law of attraction at work, you might not even appreciate it for what it is.

Rather than use the word "receive," it might make more sense to say our goal in Step 5 is to "recognize." Recognize what the law of attraction has brought into your life, and recognize where (or from Whom) those blessings came from in the first place.

What makes the law of attraction great is gratitude for your blessings. Don't forget who gives all good things. There is not much joy and peace receiving a blessing with a sense of entitlement rather than genuine gratitude for what you have.

BIBLE VERSES AND AFFIRMATIONS RECEIVE

Psalm 84:11 For the Lord God is our sun and our shield. He gives us grace and glory. The Lord will withhold no good thing from those who do what is right.
Affirmation: Thank you God for all good things!

1 Samuel 12:24 But be sure to fear the Lord and faithfully serve Him. Think of all the wonderful things He has done for you.
Affirmation: Thank you, Lord, for faithfully blessing me. I will faithfully work toward achieving Your plans for me.

Psalm 23:1 The Lord is my shepherd, I have everything I need
Affirmation: I am wise with the gifts God gives me, knowing everything is His, and He will supply all my needs.

John 1:3 God created everything through Him, and nothing was created except through Him.
Affirmation: I know where my blessings come from and thank God every moment of every day!

Psalm 100:4 Enter with the password: "Thank you!" Make yourself at home, talking praise. Thank Him, worship Him.
Affirmation: Thank you, God, for it all! The excitement, the fear, the anticipation, the blessings. You are the best!

1 Chronicles 16:24 Publish his glorious deeds among the nations. Tell everyone about the amazing things He does.
Affirmation: I never stop sharing God's amazing goodness with others through my actions as well as my words.

Psalm 118:129 Give thanks to the Lord, for He is good! His faithful love endures forever.
Affirmation: Thank you, Lord! Your love is what keeps me going. I will keep at it forever because you love me forever.

1 Timothy 4: 4-5 For everything God created is good, and nothing is to be rejected if it is received with thanksgiving because it is consecrated by the word of God and prayer.
Affirmation: Thanks to God for all things! Even when I can't see how it will work out in my life, I know God is good, and all things work together according to His plan.

Psalm 28:7 The Lord is my strength and my shield; my heart trusts in Him, and He helps me. My heart leaps for joy, and with my song I praise Him.
Affirmation: Praise be to God! I conquer all challenges through God's strength!

Psalm 106:1 Praise the Lord. Give thanks to the Lord, for He is good; His love endures forever.
Affirmation: Praise and thanksgiving that God never leaves my side.

7
PART 6: POSITIVE MENTAL ATTITUDE (PMA)

In Positive, optimistic thinking is the building block for each of the five steps of God's law of attraction. If we can think in a positive manner most of the time, we will come a long way in our quest to become more actively patient with our circumstances. W. Clement Stone calls this positive mental attitude "PMA."

When dealing with circumstances that seem out of our control, we will all have the occasional negative thoughts. Nevertheless, constantly dwelling on the negative side of the equation will not help us. It just gives Satan a more fertile field to plant his seeds. Our thoughts are what drive our emotions, and negative and irrational thinking will lead to unhealthy emotional states. Here are some final affirmations to help shape your thought patterns to be more positive and less negative.

BIBLE VERSES AND AFFIRMATIONS: PMA

Ephesians 4:29 Let everything you say be good and helpful so that your words will be encouragement to those who hear them.
Affirmation: I speak encouraging and motivating words so that everyone who hears (including myself) is inspired.

Matthew 5:22 If you are even angry with someone, you are subject to judgment!
Affirmation: I lovingly see the good in all people and curb my anger against them.

Proverbs 4: 23 Guard your heart above all else, for it determines the course of your life.
Affirmation: I honor my hopes and dreams and work to satisfy them to God's glory. I never let others steal my dream.

Matthew 6:12 And forgive us our sins, as we have forgiven those who sin against us.
Affirmation: Because God forgives my many sins instantly, I am fast to forgive others.

Proverbs 13:3 Those who control their tongues will have a long life; a quick retort can ruin everything.
Affirmation: I think before speaking and strive to be wise in all I say.

Psalm 103:8 The Lord is compassionate and merciful, slow to get angry and filled with unfailing love.
Affirmation: I am kind and patient with others because God is kind and patient with me.

1 Thessalonians 5:18 Be cheerful no matter what; pray all the time; thank God no matter what happens. This is the way God wants you, who belong to Christ Jesus, to live.
Affirmation: I am cheerful and thankful all the time.

Romans 8:31 What shall we say about such wonderful things as these? If God is for us, who can ever be against us?
Affirmation: Leave Satan! If God is for me – no one can be against me!

Proverbs 3:3-4 Never let loyalty and kindness leave you! Tie them around your neck as a reminder. Write them deep within your heart. Then you will find favor with both God and people, and you will earn a good reputation.
Affirmation: I am faithful and kind to others because God has always been faithful and kind to me.

Romans 12:2 Don't copy the behavior and customs of this world, but let God transform you into a new person by changing the way you think. Then you will learn to know God's will for you, which is good and pleasing and perfect.
Affirmation: I focus on healthy, positive thoughts over worry and doubt. I am at peace and ready to hear what God has in store for me!

Luke 17:21 You won't be able to say, 'Here it is!' or 'It's over there!' For the Kingdom of God is already among you.
Affirmation: I am in God's hands. He is here, with me, all day today, through everything I will face.

1 Timothy 6:12 Fight the good fight for the true faith. Hold tightly to the eternal life to which God has called you, which you have confessed so well before many witnesses.
Affirmation: I am persistent and patient in pursuing God's plan for my life.

Romans 12:12 Rejoice in our confident hope. Be patient in trouble, and keep on praying.
Affirmation: With every prayer, there's fresh hope!

Galatians 2:20 It is no longer I who live, but Christ lives in me. So I live in this earthly body by trusting in the Son of God, who loved me and gave himself for me.

Affirmation: I am God's creation. Christ is in me, and I believe and trust He will guide my ways today!

1 Timothy 4:12 Don't let anyone think less of you because you are young. Be an example to all believers in what you say, in the way you live, in your love, your faith, and your purity.

Affirmation: I am a reflection of God's love and commitment in what I do and say each day.

John 3:16 For God loved the world so much that He gave His one and only Son so that everyone who believes in Him will not perish but have eternal life.

Affirmation: I am God's child, and he loves me and forgives me! I in turn love and forgive the people in my life.

2 Timothy 4:7 I have fought the good fight, I have finished the race, and I have remained faithful.

Affirmation: I live every day in a way so that I can lay my head down and say: I have fought the good fight, I have finished the race, and I have remained faithful. Thanks be to God!

ABOUT THE AUTHOR

As the wife of a small business owner and the mother of two, Susan Lee has discovered that it's never too late to grasp God's plans as our own and experience His best. She hopes that through her writing she can help others to discover God's unique plan for their lives and to Live Large For God! Connect with Susan Lee at ProduceMyBook.com/gloabonusreg

While this is the end of the book, I hope you will stay in touch! If you enjoyed Experiencing God's Law of Attraction Through Bible Verses and Spiritual Affirmations, please take the time to give me a review. Very few people take the time, so it is a really big deal if you do. I very much appreciate it. To leave a review, please visit my Author page on amazon.com/author/susanleebooks

Please connect with me at ProduceMyBook.com/gloabonusreg, or email me at crew@ProduceMyBook.com

Be sure to visit **ProduceMyBook.com** to learn how you can FINALLY get the book inside you written and produced!

ProduceMyBook.com: Concept to customer non-fiction books in as little as 8 weeks without the author ever typing a word of the manuscript!

Recommended Reading:

God's Law of Attraction: The Believer's Guide to Success and Fulfillment, By Susan Lee Available on Amazon.com

Developing Patience and Perseverance in an Impatient World, by Susan Lee Available on Amazon.com

Devotionals Reflecting on God's Power: What the Bible Teaches Us About Praise, Forgiveness, and More, by Susan Lee Available on Amazon.com

FREE BONUS!

Don't Forget to download your free bonus!

God's Law of Attraction Worksheets which will help you determine your goals, create positive affirmations, and combat negative beliefs.

Treasury of God's Promises is a collection of Bible verses that will help you focus on God's positive message.

Quotable Quotes is a selection of affirming quotes that will help you to keep God's powerful word in your heart.

To get all three gifts, just visit **ProduceMyBook.com/gloabonusreg**

Made in the USA
Coppell, TX
15 July 2020